THE STARTING BLU PRNT

What You Can Expect When Starting A Business

Joseph A Tenuta, MBA

The BluPrnt

Copyright © 2025 Joseph A Tenuta, MBA

All rights reserved

The characters and events portrayed in this book are fictitious. Any similarity to real persons, living or dead, is coincidental and not intended by the author.

No part of this book may be reproduced, or stored in a retrieval system, or transmitted in any form or by any means, electronic, mechanical, photocopying, recording, or otherwise, without express written permission of the publisher.

ISBN-13: 9798320247687
ISBN-10: 1477123456

Cover design by: Art Painter
Library of Congress Control Number: 2018675309
Printed in the United States of America

To my wife Jenny for the consistent love and support in everything I do….

To Sophia, Audrey, JJ, Sonny, and Antonia for showing me what life is really about…

To Cesare and Antonia Tenuta for being the best parents a kid could ask for…

CONTENTS

Title Page
Copyright
Dedication
Forward
I Have An Idea! — 1
Main Building Blocks — 9
Business Structure Basics — 14
C.Y.A. — 23
Money Basics — 26

Branding — 38
You Got Mail! — 45
Know Your Market! — 48
Sell! Sell! Sell! — 54
Time for the Operator — 60
Human Capital — 65
Leverage — 69
Go! — 72

The Starting BluPrnt Checklist — 74
The Starting BluPrnt - Fun Stuff — 77

FORWARD

*Be Humble | Be Considerate |
Spend Less | Hustle More | Pray
Always – Joey Tenuta MBA*

I am scared of failure. I am scared to let people down, especially those closest to me. I am ambitious and I have a mentality to serve others. Mom and Dad were both immigrants and immigrants do not mess with work. Work was a 7-day per week ordeal. They instilled a work ethic in me like none other and, next to failure; I am motivated by the fear of regret. I have spent a great deal of time reflecting and thinking about why I choose to work a lot or why I believe in searching out opportunities. I believe it has a great deal to do with my parents and my paternal grandparents especially. My grandparents came the United States in the early 1960s. Both of them were in their sixties. Our normal is to "retire" or consider retirement when in ones in their sixties, my grandparents saw their window to the new world was quickly closing and it was now or never. They took their four sons and one daughter to move to America leaving behind their two oldest boys as they were already established. They had their reasons and decided it would be better to start over with no regrets. I could not imagine my wife and me picking up our family and moving to a country where we do not know the language with limited resources nowadays. That is what makes our story so remarkable. For my grandparents it was an opportunity for a better life more so for their kids and especially for their future grandchildren. As one of those grandchildren, they were right.

I believe in work. Meaningful work. Work that causes you to give up on sleep, going out, partying, relaxing, and working out. You will only be able to sustain if you grow and growth takes work. This book represents growth for me. This book is not a memoir that tells the reader what I accomplished as I am still a student myself and I have a lot yet to accomplish. This book details what I am doing. What I will continue to do. I wanted to write this book because I believe that there are so many people, especially college students that have so many great ideas but do not know how to start. I hope the pages ahead inspire you to finally pursue a passion, follow a dream, serve others, or build something of your own. As my parents inspire me still every day, I hope these pages inspire you to start.

Joey Tenuta, MBA
@joeytenutamba

I HAVE AN IDEA!

"Truth is like poetry...and no one fucking likes poetry" From the film - "The Big Short"

The Starting BluPrnt is a tool I wish I had back in 2005. Back then, I was an inside sales rep for a manufacturer's rep in Southeastern Wisconsin. Only two years out of engineering school, I quickly found myself looking for more. As an inside guy, I worked 40 hours a week at my desk, learning a variety of applications, understanding processes, and quickly becoming "good at my job." I also knew I wanted more so I applied to graduate school and started thinking of what things I can do "on the side." I can distinctly recall attending a particular training event and receiving a business padfolio. Disinterested with what was going on in the training, I analyzed that padfolio and saw the name of the manufacturer embossed on it. I went to my hotel room and after some internet due diligence, I found the manufacturer, learned how to start a LLC, and became a distributor of promotional products. Joey Tenuta LLC was incorporated in 2005 and it is still in existence today but I have moved on from selling promotional products. I do still have the padfolio in my mom's basement in case you were wondering.

Over the past 19 years I have painstakingly researched, attempted, failed, and succeeded at various business ventures. Accumulating a stack of *Idea Books* each venture provided me with a lesson that I hold on to this day. *The Starting BluPrnt* will go through those lessons so you, the reader, can understand or at least appreciate the act of starting a venture of your own. No matter how small or large. One founder or multiple. No matter how advanced or boring.

What this book is, more than anything, is a way for you to understand and expect what is ahead of you when you start something. Many people fail to take the first step because they are simply afraid of not knowing what is ahead of them. They are not aware of what incorporating means, what an EIN number is, how to create a marketing plan, or even how to talk to their customers. They become overwhelmed and there is no better way to stop someone in their tracks than to overwhelm them. It takes a certain type of person to push through being overwhelmed. A person with resourcefulness, a strong work ethic, and who is very goal oriented is likely to push through. A driven, persistent person (for whatever reason) will always keep going.

This book is not a promise or a blueprint for success. You, yourself, have to define what success means to you as it will be different to everyone. Some people deem money as a measure of success; some strive for title and power, while others measure it by how much time they have for living. It is up to you to define it. This book does make one promise however. Everyone's definition will have one thing in common and that thing is work.

So why do it? Why voluntarily sign up for a painful, stressful, long, and unnerving experience? The truth is that we are all built differently. Some of us see opportunities where others see roadblocks. Some of us prefer challenges where others prefer easy. Some of us sit in the front of the class and some want to hide in the back. Those of us that sign up to start something do so because we would rather go through turmoil than live with what if. What if I built that app? What if I took that leap? What if my grandfather said decided not to come to America?

Success to me is:

_____

_____

_____

Jeff Bezos (I am sure you know who he is) is famous for saying that "Big Things Start Small" and he is right. The majority of businesses start small. In March 2023, the Small Business Administration (www.sba.gov) reported that in the US alone there are over 33,185,550 small businesses in the United States. According to Forbes magazine, (www.forbes.com), if you were to add up all the businesses in the United States, small businesses would make up 99% of the businesses that are operating in the US which employ nearly 50% of the population. The United States of America, frankly, is dependent on those who wrestle up the courage to start something. The United States favors the risk takers.

If you have wanted to start something of your own, this book will be of great value to you. If you have had a passion that drives you and all you need is help off the starting line, this book will be of great value to you. If you are looking for a foolproof plan to become a millionaire in 1 year, this book is NOT for you. As Sir Winston Churchill said in his speech to the House of Commons on May 13, 1940, "I have nothing to offer but blood, toil, tears and sweat." Sir Winston Churchill's quote resonates with small business owners and founders because starting a business is a painstaking ordeal. Your life will become worse before it becomes better. You will exchange 40 hours per week with paid time off for 80 hours a week and working Holidays. If the end goal is important than sacrifices will have to be made.

Choosing to read this, there must be something inside of you that is nudging you forward. It can be all sorts of motivation. Time, money, passion, and power. The great thing about this book is how it applies to anyone at any age. It is never too late. Colonel Sanders was in his sixties when he started Kentucky Fried Chicken. Nor does it matter if you are providing products or services or even want to be an influencer. The topics in this book apply to everyone.

The only prerequisite is the willingness to work. I often have to remind my teenagers that roam my home that Mr. Beast did not become a sensation overnight. He put his 10,000 hours in and continues to do so. He's fanatic about work. His computer is next to his bed, he rarely takes time off, and he often works until he reaches the point of exhaustion or burn out. Make sure you ignore the videos and posts that say how success is easy. Flashes of success may happen but sustainable, long-term success will not be. There is no magic wand and so many will not care about the work you are putting in. If you happen to make it, those same people will think you waved a magic wand and try to discredit you.

Below are some anecdotes and notions to keep in mind as you ready yourself for the start. If you have a hard time digesting these, then you will have an even more difficult time ahead of you and a high probability of failure.

There will never be a perfect time to start. You have to decide at what point you want to start betting on yourself instead of waiting for others to get you where you want to be.

You need a thick skin. You may think your idea is great, others will not. There will be naysayers and critics. You cannot let it bother you or deter you. You must be your number one believer.

Talk to your spouse or partner. When people begin a business, their home life feels it first and hardest. A stable home means better focus and less guilt. If the home becomes contentious, it will affect the business.

If you are leaving a "job" to do your own thing, understand that you are leaving a boss for a new "boss". That new boss is your customer. What they say goes.

If you are leaving a "job", understand that you are giving up a salary, a typical work schedule, possibly health insurance, likely a retirement plan and paid time off for an uncertain salary, twice the workload, and no time off. Especially in the beginning.

Be comfortable being alone. Physically and mentally. You cannot expect everyone around you to understand, appreciate, or care what you are going through. You have to be able to handle the challenges both physically (oftentimes with no sleep) and mentally.

Be patient. Things will not go as planned. There will be twists and turns, unexpected problems, and hurdles. If you believe in it, you have to be patient about it.

When your fears are greater than your Faith, you will feel like your life is a mess.

Understand where your time is spent. There is a finite amount of time in a day. You are the master of it. Spending it wisely is vital. Doom scrolling has to go. You may have to sacrifice leisurely activities. Or wake up earlier than normal to get things done.

There is no longer "work-life" balance. Stop saying it, wanting it, thinking about it. Your life will be out of balance.

Failure will slap you in public but success only hugs you in private.

You will need patience when you have nothing and the right attitude when you have everything.

Comparison is the thief of your joy so focus on your own accomplishments.

Be comfortable being uncomfortable. You will have to step out of your shell. Take the initiative to introduce yourself and your company to strangers. Work with customers, partners, vendors, and competitors. You will have to make hard decisions and you will piss people off. It is time to get off the sidelines and in the game no matter how uncomfortable it is for you.

Do not discredit taking some inventory of yourself especially regarding how much risk to handle. College students are at a great advantage when starting a business because dorm living and the Affordable Care Act take care of key necessities one needs in life. When you have a family, spouse, mortgage, and need insurance, you tend to be more risk averse. Understanding what you can handle before your start can save you a lot of stress and turmoil.

Quick Note: At the end of each chapter, you will find a checklist of action items discussed in chapter along with key terms and definitions. Complete each task the best you can and note the key terms to reference later on. Do not be discouraged if you cannot complete all the items on the checklists. You can always come back to them when you can.

End of Chapter Checklist

What is my idea?

What do I truly want to do?

Have I spoken to my spouse/partner?

List 5 people to share your idea with?

What feedback did I get?

What am I okay with giving up?

What am I not okay with giving up?

Where do I envision myself in 5 years? 10 years?

Here is a short video of me talking about ideas!

MAIN BUILDING BLOCKS

Perfect love drives out fear...1 John 4.18

I have fond memories of my childhood. Best parents a boy could ask for. They checked all the boxes. Endearing, compassionate, empathetic, hardworking, fair, loving, and motivating. Both immigrants, hard work was instilled in their DNA. They raised my brothers and I to be productive, hardworking, family men. They raised us with strong values. I have four older brothers, all a few years older than me so when I came into adolescence, they were out beginning their own lives. Regardless of the age differences, the values were the same. Our parents set a vision of what this family is about and we all bought in.

Now that you are ready to start, the first step is to take some "pen to paper" and draft your mission, vision, and values. The immediate reaction I typically get is that there is a lot to be done and why waste time on some jargon. So many people are caught by this oversight. Your mission, vision, and values produce your north star as you begin to navigate the startup landscape.

The mission statement verbalizes why you are in business. It lets every client, employee, stakeholder know what your company is about. For example, everyone knows what Google is. Their mission is to organize the world's information and make it universally accessible and useful. I think they did that. Do you know anyone that does not "Google" a topic, question, or something else? Merriam Webster actually lists "googles" as a transitive verb meaning to use the Google search engine to obtain information about someone or something on the World Wide Web.

This will take some time but it is critical to the success of your business. To help, ask yourself "why" 5 times. Say you would like to open up your own neighborhood deli.

First Why: I have family recipes that are delicious and I know people will love.

Second Why: My family has been part of this community for years.

Third Why: I really enjoy cooking for people.

Fourth Why: My neighborhood needs a place where they can gather and get what they need.

Fifth Why: I have a passion to do something that serves my community and benefits my family.

Your Mission: To serve our neighborhoods through food and strengthen our community.

Merely an example and you may not find that inspiring but let us break it down.

> To serve: letting people know that your plan to serve or to be of service to someone, you are telling them I will take care of you. You will see them at the counter. You will remember their name. You will smile and say good morning. It becomes personal.
>
> Our neighborhoods: The plural leaves it open. Say, things go well, you want to expand and serve more neighborhoods, you will, and your mission remains true.
>
> Through food: You are feeding people and/or providing ancillary items the community needs and like a deli would. Fulfilling the area's needs conveniently.
>
> Strengthen Our Community: You are saying that your business will operate and employ people from within. Providing stability and maybe inspiring others to do the same.

Holding on to that mission, you will operate accordingly. Selling items that your customers need. Providing menu items that they are looking for, understanding price points and where pricing needs to be. You will keep this mind when working with vendors. You may find yourself hiring from the local high school. Supporting the Little League team. Sponsoring a local event. Your mission becomes a guide for every facet of your business. The mission lays the tracks for which your business will run on.

The mission statement sets the tone as to what you do. Your vision statement will state how you are going to do it. Go back to Google. Their vision statement is <u>to provide access to the world's information in one click</u>. They clearly stated that they wanted to organize the world's information and make it accessible. They are going to do it with one click. That is what they are doing. We have all typed a topic or question and hit the search button. Their home page is doing what they set out to do.

A neighborhood delicatessen is not a tech company and is much smaller in scope lest not anyone think that a vision statement is less important. A vision statement for a neighborhood deli may be brief:

> Building a community one sandwich at a time.

> or

> Serving our neighbors each day with great food.

"One sandwich at a time" or "serving our neighbors each day" may not be perfect though you can get the picture. As you think about what you are setting out to do, detail your vision so that others know what you are planning on doing and how.

The last piece of this part of your start is to determine what your core values are. These are guiding principles that determine how you act as an organization. Some may consider them buzzwords or corporate jargon. When you use them and apply them, they become values. A word of warning, you may find yourself getting carried away. Limit your core values to 4 - 5 and that is it. Let us close the loop with Google shall we. Their core values are:

> Respect the user |Respect the opportunity | Respect each other

Their values tell us that we can expect a good experience when dealing with them no matter the situation. For our deli, their values could be:

> Honesty | Service | Respect | Welcoming

If you think about walking into a deli and the owner greets you with a smile, makes you feel welcomed, learns your name, listens to your needs and wants, they are applying these core values.

When your core values define your beliefs, they guide your decisions and you have now created a strategy with a common thread that establishes your company's culture.

End of Chapter Checklist

Mission:

Vision:

Core Values:

Key Terms

Mission Statement: a formal summary of the aims and values of a company, organization, or individual.

Vision Statement: a written declaration clarifying your business's meaning and purpose for stakeholders, especially employees.

Core values: the ingrained principles that guide all of a company's actions

BUSINESS STRUCTURE BASICS

All hard work brings profits but mere talk leads only to poverty... Proverbs 14 v 23.

Congratulations on your new pursuit. I hope you have your mission, vision, and core values locked in. Let us roll up our sleeves. We are starting with business structure and it is important to know what they are and which one suits your personal situation best. Many aspiring entrepreneurs will not know about corporate structures and the nuances surrounding each of them. Many hear the term 'CEO' and we assume rich, intelligent, and powerful. Sure, some are but in reality when you are starting, you are a *Chief Everything Officer*. There is something profound when you say that you are the owner, President, or Founder of a company but saying it is far different from being it. You are 100% responsible for everything that goes in and around your business. From staff to sales to finance and debt, everything falls to you. It is not a job for the meek. A proper understanding of how a company is structured is paramount.

Corporate structures exist for several, important reasons. They offer legal protection to the owners and/or shareholders of the corporation. They are entitled to take advantage of tax benefits offered by the Government. They also provide perpetual existence meaning they corporation will continue to operate in the event of ownership change or death of the owners. The first company incorporated in the United States was the Massachusetts Bay Company in 1629. Massachusetts Bay was established by a group of English Puritans with the intention of creating a settlement in the New World. They played a significant role in the colonization of what would later become the Massachusetts Bay Colony, a key early settlement in what is now the United States. At of the end of 2020, in the United States, the U.S. Census Bureau's Business Formation Statistics reports, there were approximately 32.5 million businesses. This includes both employer and non-employer businesses. Nearly 400 years later the corporate structure provides a framework for operating a business but the specific structure you choose should align with your goals, size, and nature of your business.

Corporations: A corporation is a legal entity that is separate from its owners. It is a legal business entity created by individuals, stockholders, or shareholders to operate for profit. Corporations are governed by the state in which they are registered to act as a single entity. They have many of the same rights and responsibilities as individuals, including:

Entering into contracts

Suing and being sued

Owning assets

Remitting federal and state taxes

Borrowing money from financial institutions

Hiring employees

Sole Proprietorship: A sole proprietorship is a one-person enterprise and any revenue and tax liability is tied directly to the owner (i.e. their social security number). Any liability falls to the owner and any personal assets are at risk.

Take the traditional lemonade stand. You set up a stand and people love your Aunt Mae's old-fashioned lemonade recipe. You incorporate as a sole proprietorship and you keep detailed financials. No issues with reporting income and paying taxes. One day, a customer gets sick and they claim that it was the lemonade that made them ill. You are then slapped with a lawsuit and they are looking to sue you for damages, pain, and suffering. Your personal assets are at risk. There is no corporate veil. A corporate veil is a legal concept that separates the personality of a corporation from the personalities of its shareholders. It protects you, the owner, from being personally liable for the company's debts and other obligations.

Partnerships: Partnerships are similar to the sole proprietorship with the exception that there is more than one person involved or owning the enterprise. Same liabilities apply and no corporate veil exists.

C-Corporation: A C-corporation (or C corp) is a legal structure for a corporation in which the owners, or shareholders, are taxed separately from the entity. They offer the strongest protection to its owners from personal liability, but the cost to form a corporation is higher than other corporate structures. C-corps are also subject to paying its share of taxes resulting in what is known as double taxation.

S-Corporation: An S corporation protects the personal assets of its owner(s). Absent an express personal guarantee, a shareholder is not personally responsible for the business debts and liabilities. Creditors cannot pursue the personal assets (house, bank accounts, etc.) of the shareholders to pay business debts.

A Limited Liability Company: A limited liability company (LLC) is a corporate structure and is very popular because they limit the personal liability of their owners. Unlike stock in a C-corp, owners of LLCs hold membership units and are often referred to as members. This means that in the event of bankruptcy or lawsuit, the personal assets of the LLC's owners and members are protected from any business liability.

A Limited Liability Partnership: A Limited Liability Partnership (LLP) is a general partnership where each partner has limited personal liability. LLPs are a cross between a corporation and a partnership. The best way to think of a LLP is that partners are not liable for the debts or claims of the partnership. They are also not liable for the tortious damages of other partners. If one partner makes an error, the other partners are not liable for their error.

When you are starting out, the most common corporation is a limited liability company. All my enterprises are LLCs. They are a bit more involved and expensive than a sole proprietorship but you can protect your personal assets with an LLC. Limited liability companies are governed by the State where they are registered in. Some states make it easier to incorporate while other states make it more difficult.

All but one of my LLCs were incorporated in house meaning I did them on my own. The State of Wisconsin makes it pretty easy to start an LLC right from the Department of Financial Institutions website. Through the website, you can quickly do a name search to see if there are any LLCs already registered with the name you intend to use. If there are currently active LLCs with the name you intended to use, you will need to find a new name. If not, you are free to begin the incorporation. You will need the contact information of all the members (i.e. owners) of the LLC along with the primary address of the LLC, and the contact of who will be the registered agent. The registered agent is simply the person who will receive correspondence from the State and will be notified when it is time to renew the LLC with the State. LLCs must be renewed yearly. Once the form is submitted, you can expect a response from the State notifying you that the form was received. If there are no issues or missing information, you will receive a second notice stating that your LLC has been filed. With that notice, you will be provided your Article of Incorporation. You will need those as they list all the pertinent information of the business and have the official incorporation date listed. Keep a hard copy and an electronic copy. Additional copies are available through the State for an additional fee in the event they are lost or damaged.

Do not be discouraged if this whole process seems overwhelming to you. It can be for some. The thought of self-lawyering can be unnerving. If you are such a person, I would highly recommend seeking out an attorney in your town to help. They will likely be very affordable and can act as your registered agent so you are renewed every year. If you Google "starting my own LLC" please be forewarned that you will be inundated with ads from online companies scattered throughout the world that promise to do it for free and easy and quickly. There may be viable companies that do this but if you do not want to do it yourself, lean on a local human being to help you. They can advise you and provide guidance that is based on your situation. You will rest easier working with an actual person if you need to.

While you are waiting for the State to return your application and file your company, you can begin working on your LLC operating agreement. An operating agreement is a document that outlines the terms of a limited liability company. It is a written agreement between members of an LLC that is similar to a partnership agreement. It is a necessity for an LLC that has multiple members and its good practice to have one if you are a sole-member LLC meaning it is just you. The operating agreement stands to be the rules by which the LLC operates. It will dictate how decisions are made, how losses and profits are distributed, and what percentage of the LLC each member owns. I have an LLC where there are three members. Our operating agreement outlines how we have to have a majority vote for decisions. It states that one member cannot take out a loan or make a larger purchase through the company without each member's consent. Stipulations that are there to protect the members and the LLC.

> A special note for college students in Wisconsin. The Governor's Office has a special program for college entrepreneurs. If a student is a full time student, they can file their LLC and the State will waive their filing fee! It is a great way to get started and save a little cash as well.

Again, I personally did some self-lawyering on my operating agreements. There are plenty of templates to be found online as long as you are cautious and trust the source. If you would prefer, a lawyer that is willing to help you incorporate will easily be able to generate an operating agreement for your business quickly. It is second nature for them. A small fee for their services may give you peace of mind if this is a topic you are not necessarily strong in.

The last part of setting up your business is to understand what licensing requirements are necessary by your state and/or even your local government. This is dependent on the nature of your business but it does warrant you conducting thorough due diligence (i.e. research). There are many types of licenses out there. From a bartender license to cosmetology to engineering to restaurants. It is up to you to make sure you have the correct license to operate. Do not forget you may need a permit to sell items and/or an occupancy permit if you are opening up a retail location. You will have to check with the State you live in along with the City where you operate. Every state maintains an office of licensure that will provide current, ample information to you regarding the specific license(s) your company will need to operate. You do not want to start operating without licenses because you your operation will cease rather quickly.

A note about lawyers. I am not anti-lawyers. I actually love lawyers. I have two in my family. The need for legal counsel will depend on the complexity of your business. If you are selling tacos out of a truck, you may not need ongoing legal guidance. You may need to make sure you are set up correctly and good to operate. Periodic "check-ins" should suffice. If your business is producing a healthtech software that is a subscription for a service model, you will need more legal help to establish different terms, policies, and contracts. At the end of the day, having an attorney you can trust will be worth it especially if you are understanding of what your particular needs are. They can help you complete all the necessary steps that you need to complete in order to start and the fees you will pay upfront will be worth it.

End of Chapter Checklist

    Find an Attorney

    Incorporation

- Complete Paperwork
- File with the State
- Secure Article of Incorporation
- Draft Operating Agreement
- Licensing
- Identify Licenses Needed
- Complete License Applications
- Secure Licenses

Key Terms

Sole proprietorship: is a business owned and run by one person. The business is not a separate entity from the owner's personal assets and liabilities. This means that the owner is personally liable for all business debts, losses, and actions.

Corporate veil: is a legal term that refers to the separation between a legal entity's assets and the personal assets of its shareholders, directors, and officers

Partnership: is a voluntary, contractual agreement between two or more people to do business for profit. Partners contribute resources like money, property, labor, or skills, and share in the profits and losses of the business.

C Corporation or C corp: is a legal structure for a corporation. It's the standard corporation under IRS rules, and is the most common type of corporation.

S corporations: are corporations that elect to pass corporate income, losses, deductions, and credits through to their shareholders for federal tax purposes.

Limited Liability Company (LLC): is a business structure that combines aspects of both corporations and partnerships.

Limited Liability Partnership (LLP): is a type of general partnership where each partner has limited personal liability for the partnership's debts.

Registered agent: is a person or company that receives legal documents, official communications, and service of process on behalf of a business.

Operating Agreement: is a legal contract that outlines the structure, management, and decision-making process for a limited liability company (LLC).

C.Y.A.

The Lord's blessing brings wealth, and he adds no trouble to it...Proverbs 10 v 22

I know what you are thinking. These mundane topics like operating agreements, licenses, and Articles of Incorporation are not fun. They are not inspiring. It is not motivating. Moreover, you are right. When you are excited about starting something and the momentum is palpable, these topics can feel like dampers. In addition, there is no bigger damper than the topics of insurance and liability. The unfortunate truth is that you must protect the business and yourself personally. Before you generate revenue, you need to protect yourself.

Let us first address liability. Some businesses may not have too much. A reseller or wholesaler may not need to worry about the products they sell, as they are merely part of the distribution network. Problems with the product fall to the manufacturer. If you are a dentist and starting your own practice, the operation is more complicated. You are performing a service on a human being and can be held liable in the event something goes wrong for whatever reason.

The way you cover yourself against liability is through insurance. Specifically business insurance. This is not like the health insurance you use when you go to the doctor. This is an entirely different beast, which you need to understand. Many businesses will need a general liability policy. A general liability policy will help protect your small business from lawsuits that may arise during normal business operations. General liability insurance can cover claims such as bodily injury (medical expenses for injuries caused by a third party, such as a customer slipping and falling), property damage (injuries and property damage suffered by third parties while on your property), and advertising injury (liability for advertising mistakes or copyright infringement) and more. This type of insurance can also help pay for medical bills, legal costs, judgments, and settlements. Lastly, clients may require you to carry general liability insurance with certain coverage amounts. You can always begin with a basic policy and increase coverage amounts when/if you need to. Do not be afraid to consult an insurance agent about your specific needs.

If your business requires you to have employees, then you will need to carry worker's compensation insurance in addition to your general liability policy. Workman's compensation insurance offers two levels of protection. It protects you, the employer, from lawsuits by workers injured while working while protecting employees from accidents, injuries, and illnesses. It will cover medical expenses, lost wages, and other expenses if an employee is injured on the job. It is an absolute must and your insurance agent will be able to hold your hand with selecting the appropriate coverages.

Certain businesses that provide professional services to customers, such as accountants, architects, engineers, lawyers, consultants, and counselors should consider professional liability insurance in addition to the general liability policy. Professional liability insurance, also known as errors and omissions insurance, protects your business and employees from lawsuits and claims related to errors made while providing services or advice. It can cover costs associated with lawyer fees, judgements, and settlements.

This is just the tip of the iceberg when discussing business insurance. You may need cybersecurity, commercial auto insurance, product liability insurance, and/or commercial property insurance. It all depends on the nature of your business. Do yourself a favor and find an agent that you can speak to and find the policy or policies that fit your business. No one likes the idea of a lawsuit but protecting yourself, your business, and your employees is an absolute must.

End of Chapter Checklist

    Find an Insurance Agent

    Secure General Liability Policy

    Secure Workman's Compensation Insurance (if needed)

    Secure Professional Liability Insurance (if needed)

Key Terms

General liability, also known as business liability insurance: protects businesses from claims that result from normal business operations.

Professional liability insurance, also known as Errors and Omissions (E&O) insurance: protects a business from financial losses due to claims that professional services or advice caused harm to a client or customer.

MONEY BASICS

The plans of the diligent surely leads to profit, and everyone who is hasty, surely rushes to poverty. Proverbs 21 v 5

Business finances are separate from your personal finances. It is important to understand the nuances between to the two and one major rule: Do not mix personal funds and business funds.

Between 1996 and 2000, the Enron Corporation was the darling of Wall Street that ended up in ruins in 2001. Enron executives engaged in unethical and fraudulent practices, including the commingling of personal and business funds, to manipulate financial statements and inflate the company's stock price. While employees lost their jobs, and investors suffered significant financial losses, its executives made off with millions until US investigators caught up with them. While this fraud is one of the largest corporate perpetuated fraud in the US, the lessons learned are applicable to all businesses regardless of size.

Recall previously we spoke of the corporate veil. When you mix personal funds and business funds or "commingle" funds, you have now provided an opportunity for a claim to pierce the corporate veil. For example, if you are facing a lawsuit and the attorney for the person suing you learned that you are paying your personal expenses with company funds, they now may have the opportunity to go after your business <u>and</u> you personally. To keep someone coming after you personally, keep personal funds separate.

Your business funds will have to have a home of their own. This means an operating account, which is a checking account for your business. To do this you would need to acquire your business's employer identification number through the IRS (www.irs.gov). It is free and it takes no time for businesses operating in the United States. You will need your Articles of Organization and the owner or owner's social security number.

You have likely had or currently had a job where you exchange your time for a paycheck. You receive your check every two weeks, for instance, and you are shown your gross pay, tax withholdings, and net pay. Your employer is withholding your taxes and at the end of the year, you are issued a W2 to show the total amount withheld or paid in taxes. This is common for most people. It is different for the owners of the business. Most business owners do not take a "paycheck" every two weeks. They pay themselves typically at the end of each month through what is referred to as a Member's Draw. A member's draw in an LLC is when an owner withdraws money from their business for personal use. LLC owners pay themselves through an owner's draw, which is a percentage or a fixed amount of money taken from the business's profits. A member's draw allows business funds to become personal funds that allows you, the owner, to do what you wish. Member draws are reported on the company's financials and are easily reported to the IRS for tax filing. It is just as common for business owners not to take a member's draw or forgo being paid for a period of some time. As the owner, you will have to have your eye on your company's cash flow and make sure the company is well funded to handle upcoming expenses.

Cash Flow Situations and When to Possibly Pay Yourself

Revenue (sales) has been consistent for three or more months. You have sales in progress and more in the pipeline. There is enough cash in the operating account to cover business expenses for 6 or more months. You do not wish to invest all or more in the business. - **You likely could take a portion of the profits in a member's draw.**

Revenue (sales) have been inconsistent for 3 or more months. You have some prospects but fear the sales pipeline is drying up. There is enough cash in the operating account to cover business expenses for 1 to 2 more months. You would like to invest in more advertising to drive sales. - **You likely should not take a member's draw.**

Revenue has slowed and there has been a flat line in revenue. You need to invest time and money to drive sales. Cash is about to run out and you will not have enough to cover expenses. - **You cannot take a member's draw and you will likely have to put money in.**

There are instances where owners can receive a paycheck and their taxes withheld like an employee's would. To do this, you would have to elect an S corp status and file form 2553 with the IRS. If the whole process is becoming daunting and overwhelming for you, you can consider hiring a Certified Public Accountant. Similar to a lawyer, they will be able to work with you and help you navigate the complexities and hurdles you will face when managing your company's finances. They will also be able to handle tax questions, tax filings, and identifying tax benefits that may be afforded to you. Simply, it is a good thing to have a CPA in your corner and well worth their fee.

With a your freshly minted EIN number, Articles of Incorporation, and driver's license to the bank of your choice and open a business checking account or operating account. Operating accounts will have different stipulations than a personal checking account. They can include minimum balances, a required opening deposit, and carry varying fee structures. Compare regional sized banks, to banks geared for business, to national banks. It pays to do your research here since you want a strong relationship with the bank that will handle your business funds.

Credit

Just like personal credit, your business will have to build a credit history. A strong credit history will allow banks to lend to you. One way to do this is with a business credit card. Paying your business expenses with a credit card and paying the balance down quickly will fast track your access for additional funding should you need it. Capital One, US Bank, Chase, and American Express all have business cards. Many mentioned have valuable rewards programs that can benefit your business through incentives for travel, hotels, airlines, goods, and services.

In the event your business calls for a larger amount of capital, you can pursue lines of credit or business loans for your needs. These are more involved and typically require a type of asset to secure them. If you own a home, the home may be used to secure the loan. Commercial loans, in most cases, have a term or length of loan of 5 years and the rates reflect the owner's credit and current market conditions.

Getting Paid

Revenue is great so ask yourself, how will my customers pay? If the answer is with a credit or debit card, then you will need a merchant account. A merchant account allows you to take credit card payments. Be warned, there is a fee for taking credit card payments. In 2023, the average fee ranged from 1.3% to 3.5% depending on several factors. Type of card, in person versus online, and the amount all play into what percentage *you* will pay. Some companies pass the fee along to their customers while others account for it within their pricing. Either way a fee will be paid. There are no shortages of merchant services companies. The financial institution that you choose may be able to offer merchant services. Companies like Square or PayPal offer a wide variety of products and services that you can sign up for too. Do your research here since you want to be able to have a method of collecting payments that is efficient for your business but fits your financial situation as well.

Invoicing your customers is another way to collect your cash. There could be situations that require you to invoice a company and a check issued to you. The most basic way to create an invoice is to use templates in Google Docs. The templates will allow you to populate your business's information, the customer's information, and the details of the transaction. It can be simply delivered to your customer. If invoicing is required, you must do the following:

    Create a Unique Invoice Number

    Reference the Customer's Purchase Order Number

    Correct Date

    Correct Client Information

    A "Remit To" address (where to send the check to)

    Correct Transaction Information (Price per Unit, Description, Total, Tax, etc)

    Sale Tax (if applicable)

Invoicing is very common in many businesses despite the rise in credit card use. It is up to you to determine if the nature of your business can be transactional with a merchant account or with invoicing. When a customer is looking to invoice you, they will ask you for a W9. This form provides your client with your Employer Identification Number (EIN), which the client will then use to report payments made to your company to the IRS. It is important to note that the information provided on a Form W-9 is for informational purposes only and does not involve any tax withholding. The form simply provides the necessary information to accurately report payments made by your client to your company to the IRS. Operations heavy on invoicing require a great deal of oversight and potential investment in a platform such as QuickBooks or Wave to help you manage. Before you select a system, you want to think about the system that best fits your business. A system similar to QuickBooks or Wave has built in tools to make running a business simpler.

Within an online portal, you can expect to:

> Create Invoices
> Track Invoices
> Track Deposits and Expenses
>
> Create Financials (Profit/Loss Statements)
> Pay Expenses
> Run Payroll (if you have employees)
> Process Credit Card Payments
> Manage Cash Flow
> Customer Relationship Management

If you expect to scale and grow, investing in a more robust system may make sense. If you intend to stay small then a simpler, more basic system would suffice. There is a cost per month to any of these systems so it pays to do your due diligence.

Operating Costs versus Start-Up Costs

Cash is King! We have heard that before. Not managing cash flow is one if not the leading cause of why businesses fail. If you are starting your own company, you need to understand the difference between operating costs and startup costs. For example, you are a physical therapist and you are going to venture out on your own and open your own practice. You found a convenient location in town and are ready to sign the lease. Before you do, you want to crunch numbers. Let us begin with startup costs. The following would be on your list:

    Down payment for the lease

    Lawyer for setting up my business

    Payment for insurance premiums

    Renovations to the site

    Equipment

    Supplies

    Computer/IT Equipment

    Signage

    Marketing Materials

    Advertisements

    Safety & PPE Supplies

This list is not comprehensive but you can see that there are a lot of moving parts to get a physical therapy clinic ready to operate Day 1. These are startup costs. Everything you need to proudly say, "open for business".

I chose physical therapy for a specific reason. The revenue comes in well after services are rendered. Say I come in and get an evaluation from you in your new practice, you process your charge or fee through a claim and my insurance pays it. My insurance will likely pay you between 14 - 45 working days from when you treated me. This means that you have to have operating capital (cash) in your operating account to pay for expenses while you wait for payments to come in. The same analysis can be applied to any business. From billing companies to distributors to restaurants, they will all have operating costs to operate. To calculate your operating costs you must first gather what expenses you have each month. Your typical business expenses may include:

- Rent
- Utilities
- Phone/Internet
- Insurance
- Software Subscriptions
- Marketing
- Supplies

Knowing your monthly expenses, multiply that by how many months you would like to have covered. For instance, if you would like 6 months where you know you have expenses covered then you will need 6 months of capital sitting in your account. To get to your ALL IN, combine your startup costs with 6 months of operating capital and you will arrive at the amount of money you, you and your partners, and/or investors will have to put into the company to get it going. Starting a business is time and capital intensive and there is no guarantee it will be successful. Understanding the amount of capital that is required and the risk is important going into it and may deter you from taking the leap. If it is too much to take on, then you may not enjoy entrepreneurship.

Proforma

It can be a complicated task to compile startup costs and operating expenses and analyze them. A comprehensive spreadsheet will guide you when estimating your investment and can easily convey the numbers to potential partners and investors. A solid proforma will include estimates on revenue, costs of goods sold, and expense. This analysis produces a clearer picture is your new business makes financial sense.

Sample Proforma

Tenuta's To - Go								
Income		1 month		3 month		12 month		Notes
	Est Food Sales	$ 100,000.00		$ 300,000.00		$ 1,200,000.00		
	Catering	$ -		$ -		$ -		
Total Income		$ 100,000.00		$ 300,000.00		$ 1,200,000.00		
Cost of Goods Sold								
	Cost of Sales	$ 24,000.00	24.00%	$ 72,000.00	24.00%	$ 288,000.00	24.00%	
	Smallwares	$ 1,100.00	1.10%	$ 3,300.00	1.10%	$ 13,200.00	1.10%	
	Total COGS	$ 25,100.00	25.10%	$ 75,300.00	25.10%	$ 301,200.00	25.10%	
Expenses								
	Business Expenses	$ 10,700.00	10.70%	$ 32,100.00	10.70%	$ 128,400.00	10.70%	
	Insurance	$ 1,500.00	1.50%	$ 4,500.00	1.50%	$ 18,000.00	1.50%	
	Licenses & Permits	$ 1,200.00	1.20%	$ 3,600.00	1.20%	$ 14,400.00	1.20%	
	Maintenance	$ 1,700.00	1.70%	$ 5,100.00	1.70%	$ 20,400.00	1.70%	
	Payroll	$ 24,300.00	24.30%	$ 72,900.00	24.30%	$ 291,600.00	24.30%	
	Taxes	$ 6,000.00	6.00%	$ 18,000.00	6.00%	$ 72,000.00	6.00%	
	Utilities	$ 2,000.00	2.00%	$ 6,000.00	2.00%	$ 24,000.00	2.00%	
	Building Expenses	$ 2,000.00	2.00%	$ 6,000.00	2.00%	$ 24,000.00	2.00%	
	Advertising & Promotion	$ 2,700.00	2.70%	$ 8,100.00	2.70%	$ 32,400.00	2.70%	
	Total Expenses	$ 52,100.00	52.10%	$ 156,300.00	52.10%	$ 625,200.00	52.10%	
Total Operating Expenses		$ 77,200.00		$ 231,600.00		$ 926,400.00		
Net Income (Loss)		$ 22,800.00	23%	$ 68,400.00	23%	$ 273,600.00	23%	

Proforma Notes:

Estimate the revenue (how many products can you sell at what price?)

If you do not have actual costs, you can use "industry averages" as a percentage. For Example: A restaurant owner strives for a food cost to be between 20% - 40% of revenue. Use the percentage to calculate a cost working backwards.

Cost of Goods Sold: These are costs occur when providing the items you are selling. Selling hamburgers, the number of buns you need to buy depends on the number of hamburgers you sell. The more you sell the more you buy. Cost of goods sold or COGS are variable costs and should be kept separate from expenses when conducting your analysis.

Expenses: These are costs that you will have to pay independent of revenue. They occur likely each month and your revenue will have to cover them. These are commonly known as fixed cost and have their own place in your analysis.

Runway

In the simplest way to think of it, your company's runway is the amount of time your company can continue operating before it runs out of cash. Runway is a key indicator your company's viability. It will help you make informed decisions about growth, sales, and longevity. To calculate your runway:

Take the amount of cash on hand and divide it by your total monthly expenses.

Breakeven

Every company despite type should know what their breakeven point is. This is where revenues equal total costs. The good news is that you are not losing money. The bad news is that you are not profitable. If you live off your profits then you can expect not being paid. To calculate your breakeven:

Total Revenues = Total Fixed Costs plus Total Variable Costs

When you are just starting out, knowing your total fixed costs and total variable costs (total operating costs) will provide you the target for your revenue to at least break even.

Is it worth it?

I struggled as to where to place this section since this is where tough decisions are made. You may have a great idea or you see an opportunity and you believe in your gut that such a business makes sense and can provide you a path to the life you want. You

<u>must run the numbers before you actually start</u>. Before the EIN number and articles of incorporation and operating account. **If the numbers do not work out in your favor or the risk is more than you can tolerate, this particular venture may not be viable for you.** Financial analysis has a way to remove the rose-colored glass from your eyes and give you a dose of reality. It will force you to second-guess your estimates and assumptions. Do you need a physical space (brick and mortar) or can you start in your garage (Apple did)? Can you get by with spreadsheets instead of an accounting software? Should you take on a partner?

One of the hats that I where is being a Professor. I always tell my students that whenever we are analyzing or forecasting that the numbers are giving us opportunities to ask questions. Financial analysis is the catalyst for questions. I would never tell one of my students or any of the aspiring entrepreneurs I work with to give up on a dream. After all dreams do not come through while you are sleeping. What I do say is to prepare yourself as best you can so you can navigate challenges and overcome shortfalls to get you there if you choose to take on the risk. Having to be resourceful, determined, and dedicated is what is needed. Being a risk-taker and betting on yourself is what is happening. Entrepreneurs call this grit.

End of Chapter Checklist

- EIN Number
- Operating Account
- Business Credit Card
- Merchant Account (if needed)
- Start-Up Costs
- Operating Costs (Fixed Costs & Variable Costs)

Completed Proforma

Key Terms

Employer Identification Number (EIN): is a unique number assigned to a business for easy IRS identification for tax reporting purposes.

Member's draw: is when a business owner takes money from their business for personal use.

Merchant Account: is a type of business bank account that allows businesses to process electronic payments.

Cost of goods sold (COGS): is the total cost of creating or acquiring products. It is an important metric on financial statements because it is deducted from a company's revenues to determine its gross profit

Fixed costs: business expenses that remain the same regardless of a business's activity level.

Runway: the amount of time your company can continue operating before it runs out of cash.

Breakeven: where total revenues equal total costs.

Here is a link to the Proforma for you to use.

BRANDING

He who works his land will have abundant food. But he who chases fantasies lacks judgment....
- Proverbs Ch. 12 v 11

My father, Cesare Tenuta, was a great man. He took pride in everything he did. A laborer turned machinist but also a restaurateur. I recall as a young kid watching him shave or scrub the grease off his fingernails with a nailbrush for a night out or family dinner. If you were to meet him outside of work, you never knew he was a machinist during the day or made pizzas at night. Often my brothers and I would hear him say, "If you get dressed and no one notices, you did not do a good job!" To our Dad looking good meant feeling good and, in a sense, he was telling the world that it did not matter what he did for a living. The care and effort he took to look and act distinguished and courteous was his way to show others how he valued them, their time, and the relationship they shared. It was his way of messaging what his brand was.

What is a brand? A brand is the identity and story of your company that distinguishes it from its competitors. It is more than simply your company's name, logo, product, or price tag. Your brand is the sum of how your business is perceived by those who experience it, including customers, investors, employees, and the media. The goal of your branding should be to earn space in the minds of the target audience and become their preferred option for doing business. The best brands reduce risk involved in the buying process and increase information efficiency.

A great example of a brand is Apple. From a compelling start up to a stock market juggernaut, Apple's brand is rooted in why they do what they do. Apple's mission is to create best-in-class technology products and services that enrich the lives of its customers. This is what Steve Jobs set out to do when he co-founded Apple Computers. Apple users often boast about the quality, ease of use, and/or features of their products. Through a combination of innovation, design excellence, user experience, quality, and marketing prowess with a consistent brand identity, Apple resonates with consumers worldwide.

> *Special Note: People do not buy what you do; they buy why you do it. – Simon Sinek*

I personally believe a brand is your company's promise to its customers, employees, and investors. Apple promises state of the art products. McDonald's promises a hot meal in a short time for a low price. Nike promises quality products for the serious athlete. What is your promise?

My Company _____

promises to _____.

Your company's promise is the first component to your company's brand identity. Thinking of your brands identity, it is your responsibility to develop:

- Your Brand Story
- Brand Personality
- Visual Identity
- Communication Style
- Product or Service
- Brand Name

When your brand is based on your values and your actions demonstrate your values, you have created the right culture.

Logo

A logo is a key part of a business's branding strategy. It is a visual representation of your company's identity, values, and mission. A well-designed logo can help your business:

- Stand out
- Build recognition
- Separate from competition

Create emotional connections
Improve memorability
Foster loyalty

Creating a logo is a fun process but can be daunting. To guide you in designing a memorable logo remember to use a combination mark, which pairs an identifiable image with your brand name. You may also start with the familiar and build from that point. Try to shape and color the logo in a way that is memorable. If you find yourself falling short of developing a logo on your own, there are numerous ways to get assistance with creating your logo. Websites such as Free Logo Services (www.freelogoservices.com) offer free tools that will allow you to build various logos. You only have to pay for the logo that you download.

Website

Your company will need a presence on the world wide web. Creating the best website is subjective and is based on the needs of your business. Selling products online? You will likely have to invest in this a great deal. Promoting a service, you may only need a simple, effective website. There are countless resources available online that can build a site for you for all budget levels. Be sure that whichever site you develop conveys your promise to its visitors and the appearance (logo, colors, fonts) are consistent with your company's visual identity.

Landing pages are a great way to establish your footprint on the world wide web without the heavy lift of developing a full website. A landing page will provide a vehicle for you to state your mission, vision, and values along with the products and/or services you intend to provide. Most importantly it provides a way for potential customers to contact you. Today's consumers are more educated and will likely Google search your company before they buy. A new company not having a website will come off as untrustworthy and consumers will be apprehensive about doing business. Landing pages temporarily fill that void rather inexpensively.

Will you be able to start your business without a website? Yes. Will it grow? Possibly. As you grow, should you invest in one? Yes! If you are not ready to build a website, at the very minimum, secure a unique domain name for your business. A domain name is similar to a physical address, but for a website. It consists of a website name and a domain extension (.com/.net/.biz/etc). Just like a physical address, if a domain is claimed, it's the property of the registered owner. They can be bought and sold and licensed. Securing your unique one right away will guarantee that it will be available when you are ready. Don't be discouraged if you find your ideal domain name already taken. The internet has been around for years and many people hold domains just to try to sell them. If you find that your domain is taken, you can offer to buy it or find a similar domain or different extension that still conveys your brand identity. With everything in business, there is a yearly fee for your domain.

Social Media

It is now commonplace that your business will need a presence on social media. LinkedIn, Facebook, Instagram, TikTok, YouTube, and X (formerly Twitter) play a role in promoting and reaching your target audience. You may not be ready to be active on some social media sites but it makes the utmost sense to secure your "handles" or account names on all social media sites. Having them secure provides the same piece of mind as securing your website domain. There is no cost to securing these handles on the different social media platforms. Once you identify where your customers are, you can exploit that particular social media site.

Business Cards

Call me old fashioned but I am a big advocate of business cards. A certain motivation or excitement comes from seeing your name, logo, and company name on a little piece of cardboard that you willingly give out to people. The best part, it is no longer a chore to have them printed. There are services available online that will have plenty to your door in days. Many offer online tools for you to design a card that best fits your brand identity and they are often accompanied by great discounts.

> Special Note: Use LinkedIn's personal QR Code for your profile to connect with potential clients and partners on LinkedIn.

End of Chapter Checklist

- Logo
- Business Cards
- Website/Landing Page
- Social Media Accounts

Key Terms

Brand: is a product, service, or concept that sets itself apart from other products, services, or concepts. A brand's identity is unique and immediately recognizable. It can include a name, logo, or other attribute that distinguishes a business's products and services from its competitors' products.

Scan the QR Code to see my LinkedIn Page.

YOU GOT MAIL!

Whoever loves correction loves knowledge, but he who hates reproof is stupid...Proverbs 12 v 1

Communication is key. As a business owner, you will need to communicate with a large number of people. Not just your customers but partners, vendors, suppliers, bankers, and so on. There are two types of communication: Corporate and Environmental. Corporate communication is the communication that is needed for you to operate your business. Dealing with employees, consultants, advisors, employees, vendors, suppliers, etc. The types of corporate communication can include internal chats, email, and voice but it will also include generating purchase orders, shared files, online portals, and more.

Environmental communication is the communication you will need when generating revenue and servicing the revenue generation. Here the focus will be communicating with customers and having vehicles for customers to communicate with your business. The types of environmental communication can include email, customer service departments, chatbots but it will also include invoicing, customer surveys, customer portals, and more.

A very basic tool that you will need to handle both corporate and environmental communication would be an email client. Google offers free emails and if you are a very small business, then having an email address may just do the trick (yourbusiness@gmail.com). I highly recommend a more professional email address as I believe it makes your company more trustworthy and official (yourname@yourcompany.com).

Google Workspace is the best solution for this. Using the domain you secured in Chapter 5, you can set up the domain and have a robust email client that offers you a professional email address and many tools that will help you communicate. Google Workspace plans provide a custom email for your business and include collaboration tools like Gmail, Calendar, Meet, Chat, Drive, Docs, Sheets, Slides, Forms, Sites, and more. You can select a plan that fits your business and budget. I have used Workspace in multiple companies and it has been a great tool. The thing I like the most about it is the accessibility from multiple devices. You can work at your convenience, respond to customers quickly, and stay connected.

> Special Note: If your new company plans finds itself in the healthcare or financial services space, then you must understand the importance of having a secure email. You cannot get my with a general Gmail address. If you are sharing one's financial and/or health information over the web, you have to have safeguards in place. Much like business insurance, invest in a system finds you compliant.

As you work in Google Workspace and begin to get comfortable, you will realize how many ways you can take advantage of the suite of apps. Gmail offers broadcast emails, which allows you to send promotional emails and newsletters to your clients and your contacts. Within the Contacts app, using "tags" will help you track your customers. Google Meet means no Zoom subscriptions. To be fair, if you have a history of working in Microsoft, you can also consider a Microsoft 365 account that will provide you a strong email client and a slew of web-based applications. I prefer Google since you can buy and manage your domain name and build a simple website using Google.

End of Chapter Checklist

- Email Address

- Google Workspace or Microsoft 365 Account

KNOW YOUR MARKET!

He becomes poor who works with a lazy hand, but the hand of the diligent brings wealth...Proverbs 10 v 4.

Back in 2005, I began a side hustle pushing promotional products to local businesses. I jumped in with both feet with high hopes and "dreams" of making a substantial income on the side. I studied the products, understood margins, created marketing materials, drafted email blasts, and created systems to process orders. All this work and I netted two sales both to my brothers who owned businesses. Cash quickly ran out and the operation came to a halt. As I look back, I realized what I did wrong. I did not know my market. I assumed that every business was waiting for me to show up and sell them promotional products. If I were to have done my market research, I would have learned that my market was full with competitors. I would have realized that companies do not like promotional products because they are expenses and cost is the most important driver. I would have learned or searched out niches that presented an opportunity. I failed at this venture because I thought I was special instead of really knowing my market.

Research & Data

When it comes to marketing your business, you must do your research. You will need to spend a considerable amount of time conducting your research, as it will be the up most important aspect to your planning. Find out if people are willing to pay for your product or service. Are there competitors in the market place? For how long? How successful are they? How many potential customers exist in the marketplace. Find out as much as you can about your potential market. Do so both online and in-person. Evaluate what the feedback is telling you. The most successful companies often do more listening that talking. Listen to potential customers, competitors, industry experts, and mentors to acquire valuable insight. Reinforce their feedback with data to justify and/or validate and/or change your intentions. If there is no market, you should reevaluate the business you are attempting to establish. If a market does exist, this it is time to begin getting the word out.

Before we start, let us clear something up. There is a difference between sales and marketing. Sales focuses on deals (transactions) and generating revenue. Marketing focuses on creating awareness, generating leads, and building customer relationships. Understanding the difference will help you be successful in both. First, determine if you are a B2B or B2C company. B2B is business- to-business, which specifies your product or services will be purchased by businesses. B2C is business-to-consumers meaning consumers will buy services directly. This distinction will serve you in marketing appropriately. Having a billboard on a busy highway makes sense for Chick-Fil-A as they are looking to make hungry travelers aware of their food and to entice them to stop and eat. The good Lord knows I have certainly been made aware and enticed to stop at a Chic-Fil-A or two. The same billboard for Uline would not make as much sense. The likelihood of a customer driving by and feeling compelled to order packaging peanuts is very low. What does make sense to Uline is to have a comprehensive catalog in the hands of every business that needs supplies to run their business. Understanding your buyer will help you construct a plan on how to message and market to them.

A defined target market is a group of potential customers that a business aims to reach with its products or services. A target market can be separated in two main categories: Primary and Secondary. The primary market is the market segment that your product or service fits the best. The secondary market is the market segment where your product or service can be a viable option. For example, a baker who specializes in wedding cakes will market to brides-to-be as their primary market yet birthday cakes could be a secondary market.

Simply dividing a target market into primary and secondary is not enough to really narrow and concentrate your focus. Your market can be further broken down into three distinct segments:

Total Addressable Market (TAM)

Serviceable Addressable Market (SAM)

Serviceable Obtainable Market (SOM)

To illustrate this, take our wedding cake baker. They analyzed their State and found out that yearly, an average of 10,000 weddings take place. This is their TAM. Looking into it further, they learn that in the surrounding counties, 3000 weddings take place on average each year. This is their serviceable addressable market. Focusing in yet again, they find 300 weddings take place each year in their city. This is their serviceable obtainable market. The TAM is a significant market with the potential for many orders but it is highly unlikely the baker would be able to service them properly. Focusing in on the SOM the baker can better create their marketing plan to capture as much of the SOM as possible.

Marketing Must - 4Ps

Any professional marketer will tell you that they have the 4Ps burned into their head. The 4Ps of marketing are:

Product - What is your product/service?

Price - What are you selling your product/service for?

Place - Where can your customers buy your product/service?

Promotion - How will customers hear about or find your product/service?

These are the four key elements of a marketing strategy, and are also known as the marketing mix. They interact significantly with each other and are the main factors that marketers consider when creating a campaign strategy. They are key elements to promote a brand's unique value and help it stand out from the competition.

Take this time to identify the 4ps for your business.

Product: _____

Price: _____

Place: _____

Promotion:
_____

Marketing Must - SWOT Analysis

A SWOT analysis is a framework for identifying and analyzing a business's strengths, weaknesses, opportunities, and threats. The acronym "SWOT" stands for these four factors. The primary goal of a SWOT analysis is to help you make better decisions. It can help you analyze what you do best now and develop a successful strategy for the future. A SWOT analysis facilitates an understanding of the strengths and weaknesses of your business.

It encourages you to develop strategic thinking and enables you to focus on strengths and build opportunities. Take this time to work through your own SWOT analysis.

Strengths: What am I good at?

Weaknesses: Where can I improve?

Opportunities: Where can I grow?

Threats: What will get in my way?

Take this time to work a SWOT for your business.

Strengths: _____

Weaknesses: _____

Opportunities: _____

Threats: _____

End of Chapter Checklist

The 4 Ps

SWOT Analysis

TAM

SAM

SOM

Research: Great Websites to Start Your Research

US Bureau of Labor Statistics

Census Business Builder

Hoovers

Mail Chimp (For Polling Your Potential Customers)

Key Terms

Total addressable market (TAM): is the maximum amount of revenue a company can earn from its products or services. It's the total revenue opportunity for a product or service if it were to capture 100% of the market. TAM is calculated by multiplying the total number of potential customers by the average revenue per customer.

Serviceable Addressable Market (SAM): is a metric that helps businesses estimate the part of the market they can acquire.

Serviceable Obtainable Market (SOM): is a market analysis metric that estimates the portion of revenue a company can capture from a specific product segment.

SELL! SELL! SELL!

Do not love sleep, lest you come to poverty. Open your eyes and you shall be satisfied with bread...Proverbs 20 v 13

As a reminder, there is a difference between sales and marketing. Marketing focuses on creating awareness, generating leads, and building customer relationships. Sales focuses on closing deals and generating revenue. Sales is centered on relationships with clients. Sales are critical to any business and any stage. Sales are the revenue dollars that come into your business. They are the dollars that pay for expenses, fund investment for growth, and profitability. Without sales or without revenue, you will simply fizzle out. No matter how great your service or your product.

"Hey, it's Joey bag of donuts" was a phrase I heard a great deal. In 2006, as I was starting my MBA program I was given the opportunity to transition from inside sales to outside sales. I needed a fast track to landing deals and mechanical contractors were the primary target. I had a line card of products, a spreadsheet with contact information, and a car. With that, I decided I was going to create a route and drop off donuts to the contractors every week. I can recall my route as if it were yesterday.

    Monday – Milwaukee

    Tuesday – West Milwaukee

Wednesday – Madison

Thursday – West of Madison

Friday – Kenosha/Racine

I committed to this schedule racking up miles like no one's business. I kept dropping off donuts and product literature every week. Slowly, they grew to know me and what I had to offer. One job yielded another, then two more, and it kept growing. We would spend time together, do lunches, and visit the project sites. They were beginning to trust me and know me. Over the course of 13 years, I became a partner because I had their backs. Looking out for their best interests, helping them out of jams, bringing them opportunities, and being transparent. I am proud of the work I did and more proud that we are still friends to this day. If I had not invested and committed to the relationship building, I would not have had the success that I did as a sales engineer.

There is an old saying that the customer is always right. I believe that is half the case. The right customer is always right. One thing we can all agree on or should all agree on is that customers are the only ones that truly have the ability to fire you. Sam Walton, the founder of Wal-Mart, has been quoted as saying:

> "There is only one boss: the customer. And he can fire everybody in the company from the chairman on down, simply by spending his money somewhere else."

My father shared that same belief. He was a co-owner of a pizzeria with his brother. They both were factory workers during the day and spent their evenings and weekends working at the restaurant. My mother would often take me there to visit him and I recall many occasions of me having a chocolate milkshake at the counter while he waited on his customers. He did not deviate from the level of customer service. He treated everyone like gold. I asked him once why he was so nice. He proudly said, "Son, every time a customer comes to the counter, they are spending the money they worked hard for. It does not matter to me if they are the plant manager or the janitor; our customers are gold to us. And I will treat them that way every time because I don't want them going anywhere else for pizza." Very simple and yet effective and yet holds true today nearly 40 years later.

Ask yourself, how will my customer buy from me? If you are a B2C company, will your customer be purchasing products online, through traditional retail, paying with credit cards, and coming repeatedly for repeat sales? If you are a B2B company, will there be contracts, statements of work, proposals, and invoices? Will they be paying with a check or will you take credit cards? We will discuss process flow mapping in the next chapter. For now, we are focusing on selling. If you have people close to you that have made a career out of selling, interview them. They will have a lot of tidbits and nuggets to share.

For any new business owner, your marketing efforts are there to build awareness and bring potential clients into the funnel. These potential clients are considering purchasing your product or service, they are aware of your product or service, and there may be interest. Traveling down the funnel is when a potential client moves from awareness and interest to consideration and intent. There is an important nuance to note here. The consumer, your consumer is getting smarter and has more tools available. Most if not all consumers, will Google a product/service/company before they would even want to speak to a company representative. That is why branding, website, and social media have to convey your same message. A consumer will likely begin interacting with you and your company when they are evaluating their options and/or are ready to buy.

```
        Awareness

         Interest

       Consideration

          Intent
```

While the different aspects of the funnel go between sales and marketing, the result of closing the deal falls to sales. Successful businesses keep the funnel full so the flow of deals is consistent. Not filling the funnel forces the revenue to dry up rather quickly and shortens the length of your runway.

Managing customers and potential customers is getting easier and better in recent years. Customer relationship managers or CRMs have evolved to powerful robust tools. According to crm.org, in 2010, 15% of companies used CRM solutions, but by 2020, that number had increased to 97%. In addition, in 2010, CRM businesses had a revenue of just under $14 billion, but by 2020, that number had increased to about $69 billion. Finally, in 2022, the global CRM market size was valued at $64.41 billion, and is projected to reach $157.53 billion by 2030. This surge in CRM companies means more competition, affordable pricing, and products that fit all sizes of businesses. Larger companies with many employees will have their pick of CRM products with tailored features and benefits. Startups and small companies (even those solopreneurs) can select from CRMs that fit their needs and their budgets. When considering a CRM, keep in mind the following:

Customer data management: This feature allows companies to

store, clean, collect, and easily update customer information.

Integrations: Consider how the CRM will integrate with your current operations and how they work with email systems, collaboration tools, and project management.

Easy to use: Is it friendly to use and does it have mobile access?

Access: Consider if the CRM is web-based, cloud-based, or on premise.

Reputation: Strength and reputation matter.

Automation: Can it automate simple tasks?

Price: The price must fit the budget.

Even with all the options now available, if you are just starting out there may not be an immediate need for CRM. Google Workspace offers some intuitive features for managing your clients.

Email customers using templates

Google Sheet templates

Create broadcast templates

Use labels to stay organize

Use tags to organize and sort contacts

Schedule emails

Tasks /follow up items

Set reminders

Acquiring customers and closing sales will generate the vital revenue your business will need to operate. Do not get caught up in tools and systems. Let them try out your product free. Provide free access to your service for 30 days. It takes an investment of time and capital to do this. At the end of the day, make it work. The most important thing is to be relentless in finding where your customers are, making them aware of your product and/or service, and enticing them enough so they decide to buy from you.

End of Chapter Checklist

    Research CRM software and/or system

    Identify where your customers are

    Identify how you will entice your customers

Key Terms

Customer Relationship Management Software (CRM): a system used to organize and manage all interactions with customers, including potential leads, to improve customer relationships and ultimately drive sales by centralizing customer data and providing tools for effective communication and engagement throughout the customer lifecycle.

TIME FOR THE OPERATOR

Wealth gained dishonestly dwindles away, but he who gathers by hand makes it grow...Proverbs 13 v 11.

Starting a business is not easy. So far we have discussed much about setting up a business, licensing, insurance, software, marketing yet we have yet spoken about your operation. From a lawyer delivering legal services to a manufacturer producing its widget, every business has an operation.

I always recommend that you first determine your overall strategy. Most, if not all, business fall into one of three categories:

Cost
Quality
Customer Service

Understanding which strategy fits your business and its mission is crucial to your success. For example, Amazon is obsessed with customer service. It is all about the customer at Amazon and they operate as such. Getting packages the next day, not paying for shipping, getting notifications on deliveries, and making returns simple. It is so customer focused that when they ask if you want to join Prime, we jump and say "please take my money!" Walmart on the other hand has always adopted the strategy of cost. Their mission is "to be the destination for customers to save money, no matter how they want to shop". Their no-frill stores are located within the most convenient locations, they carry a large variety of products, and they aggressively negotiate with supplies for lower and lower pricing. The strategy affects everything they do. Walmart Taglines through the Years:

    1962-1988: Always Low Prices. Always.
    1988-1994: Always The Low Price. Always.
    1994-1996: Always Low Prices. Always Walmart.
    1996-1999: Better Every Day Low Prices! Always.
    1999-2007: Always Low Prices. Always.
    2007-present: Save Money. Live Better.

In Walmart's case, high salaries, above average employee benefits, inefficient systems will only cut into profit margins. Since they committed to a cost strategy, their aim for low sale prices fuel an obsession for low operating costs to maximize profits. Committing to a strategy forces you to make operational decisions that fit the strategy. Every operational decision is evaluated on its effect on the bottom line, even if it is unpopular to most people.

Holding true to your strategy, you will now determine how you will handle managing your business. The clearly established Principles of Management consist of a 4-part framework commonly referred to as the POLC framework.

    Planning
        Mission & Vision
        Strategizing
        Goals & Objectives

    Organizing
        Organization Design
        Culture
        Social Networks

Leading
    Leadership
    Decision Making
    Communications
    Group/Teams
    Motivation

Controlling
    System/Processes
    Strategic Human Resources

You have already begun building your company's framework but now you can begin to complete it. Ask yourself the following questions

What strategy are we adopting?

Proclaim your Values. How will you do business each day?

Who is/are the leader(s) in your company?

How will decisions be made? Will you have an advisory board to help guide you?

How will you communicate with your team? With your clients?

How do you plan to motivate your team? Motivate yourself?

What processes will you implement? What systems will you have in place?

The last question carries much weight; luckily, there are tools to help you develop your processes. To begin, put yourself in your customer's shoes and envision walking through the process of buying your own product or service. The simplest way to do this is to create a flowchart or a process map. It is a visualization of how to deliver the products or services to your client. The more complicated your product or service is to deliver, the more complicated and intricate your process map will be.

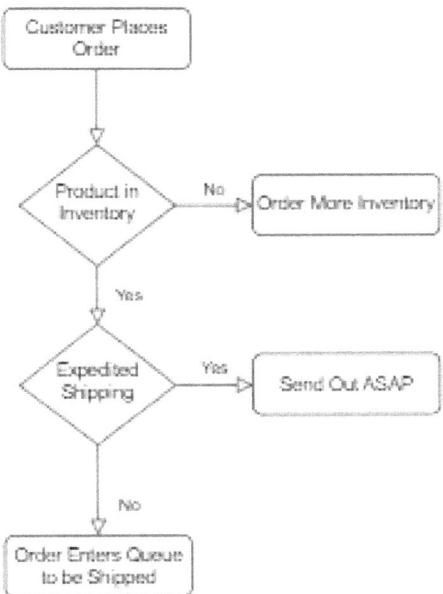

The figure above is just an example of a simple process map. As the Chief Everything Officer, it is your responsibility to sit and image what the process is. Draw it out, make changes, do test runs. Whatever it is do it before so you can get familiar for what the process entails and where potential pitfalls or "bottlenecks" are. Once of my favorite movies is *The Founder* about Ray Kroc and McDonald's. There is a scene where the McDonald's brothers explain to Ray how they designed a system to deliver a fresh cheeseburger in under 1 minute. They called it the Speedy System.

Follow the QR code and watch the clip for yourself. (I am not responsible should you head out and grab a burger).

Henry Ford famously said, "Thinking is the hardest work there is, which is probably the reason why so few engage in it." The most difficulty you will find in designing your process is the mental lift the task requires. If you are able to think it through and anticipate issues the best you can, you will be well on your way with an operational design that will support your business objectives. Mr. Ford was so good at the "process" and finding areas of improvement that many companies (even competitors) went to learn from him. Toyota, Porsche, Hermes, Firestone are among those that sought out to learn from the master. They knew he was right.

End of Chapter Checklist

What strategy are we adopting?

If you will have an advisory board, who will be on it?

How will you communicate with your team and clients?

Customer Process Map(s)

Internal Process Map(s)

HUMAN CAPITAL

Plans die due to lack of counsel but successful plans have many advisors... Proverbs Ch. 15

From 2003 to 2015, I was a sales engineer. I learned a great deal but I was never in a management positon. I was one that was managed. My oldest brother gave me a shot to be his number 2 and build a network of physical therapy clinics and a billing service. I had to take it. I recall vividly our meeting and the excitement I had after it. I called him just to say thanks once again and I will never forget what he said.

Joe, in business I bet on people, and you are a sure bet!

I know right! Talk about motivation! Once all the confetti settled, it was time to get to work, and we certainly did. We laid the foundation (mission, vision, values); we established our processes, workflows, documentation, software systems and more. We then embarked in bringing on the people that would with us. Over a period of 5 years, we grew from one employee (me) to over 100. We had established employer sponsored health insurance, retirement accounts, and other benefits to attract and retain these employees. We implemented time keeping systems, remained compliant with ACA, HIPPA, ADA, and other programs. Our foundation was solid.

I quickly learned that managing people had less to do about the systems and more to do about the actual person. It is developing a mechanism of action so you can decipher each employee's emotions and aspirations, wants and needs. It is vital to the success of your business that you get to know who you are working for. Yes, I wrote that correctly. A true leader understands they work for their employees and not the other way around. You will likely spend more time with these folks than you will your family. You can do the math.

It begins with the hiring process. Start by understanding if a qualified applicant has the same value system as you do. They will likely be the ones you trust the most and the most loyal. Next, learn and understand what they want out of life. Each person has a unique story. One may want more of a flexible schedule. Another may want more financial security. One may be hyper-focused on launching their career. It is your responsibility to know and act on these details.

As you build your business or as you realize it is time to bring on employees, consider the following items:

Do I need fulltime (40 hours per week) or part-time help?

How much can I pay them?

Will I pay them a wage, salary, or as a 1099 contractor?

Do they need to be onsite or remote?

Do I have a detailed job description prepared so they know what is expected of them?

Can I afford benefits?

What cost will go up?

What is the return on my investment in the employee?

These are very important questions that you need to ask yourself. Earlier on, I referenced an example of a physical therapy clinic. Let us go back to that. Say you are ready to hire a Patient Coordinator for your front desk. You realize your time is better spent treating patient and submitting claims rather than answering the phone and scheduling. You have a detailed job description and you have the ideal candidate. You expect them to work 8-5 Monday through Friday with an hour unpaid lunch each day. This employee is likely to be a W2 employee paid an hourly wage. This will require a paycheck every two weeks or twice a month. Taxes to be withheld and paid on their behalf. If they go over 40 hours per week, they may be entitled to 1.5 times their hourly rate. They may also be entitled to paid time off or sick time depending on the state you live in. They will need a computer, supplies, and email address, access to software, training, and coaching. You will have to make sure they understand your mission, vision, and values and they are aware of the customer service standards you want to maintain. Wait, I forgot to mention the worker's compensation insurance you will need now in the event they suffer an injury during work time. All this falls to you and your wallet.

You consider part-time help as that prevents overtime. Maybe you prefer to hire them as a contractor or 1099 employee meaning you pay them their gross wage and they are responsible for paying their own taxes. You consider outsourcing a service to answer phones and schedule appointments for a flat fee. In the end, you decide on part-time help 3 days a week. You can manage their pay but you must make sure they are trained and ready with all the equipment to do their job successfully. When it is all said and done, you can focus on development and leadership all while seeing patients.

Different businesses require different employment levels for them to function. A small barbershop will have a different need than a small coffee shop than a bakery. The more your business depends on others to complete the process that you laid out and deliver its product or service, the more you need to invest in others. You must remember you are dealing with people, their lives, livelihood, and families. The money they earn goes somewhere and they are not to be treated like a number. Especially in a small business.

Having employees is a responsibility not to be taken lightly and not to be acted upon hastily. Remember, they get paid before you do. Therefore, do your due diligence, lean in on your network, and crunch the numbers. You and your employees will be happy you did.

End of Chapter Checklist

    Do I need employee?

    If so, how many?

    What can I afford?

    Do the numbers make sense?

    Do I need people (more people) to help me grow?

LEVERAGE

If you abide in me, and my words abide in you, you shall ask what you will, and it shall be done unto you. John Chapter 15 Verse 7.

Leverage is the ability to use the resources available to you to get the results you want. As a Sales Engineer, I realized leveraging relationships was a win-win for my clients and me. It is the preverbal "I know a guy". It was extremely rewarding to bring a contractor in to a manufacturer or a hospital for an opportunity even if it meant there was nothing in it for me. If you are not surprised yet, I reflect a great deal about my Father in this book. I remember when I told him one night that I was going to go to college and study Mechanical Engineering. He was pleased and later mentioned to me that the Plant Manager of the Chrysler Engine plant was a regular. Overtime and I suspect after a great deal of conversations and free pizzas, this manager informed my Dad that I should bring him my resume when I graduated. The plant closed before I graduated but Dad was using what was around him to put someone he cared about (me) in a better position.

Successful leverage is a selfless business act that offers a great return down the road. As you are starting out, start with the people closest to you. The people that know and love you. For example, if you are starting your own baking business, every person in your family is a potential champion for you. Ask them to tell their coworkers and friends about your business. Give them samples to pass out. Ask to visit their workplaces. Ask everyone for his or her email addresses. Leverage the resources you have which will help you develop new resources and additional opportunities and the cycle continues and grows. Leverage is not "I scratch your back and you scratch mine" nor is it "I did this for you so now you have to do this for me." There is no room for pettiness when leveraging a relationship. Pettines deteriorates the foundation leverage is based on. I also am cautious not to confuse networking with leverage. Networking, in my opinion, is a valuable tool used to build awareness. Leverage is a strategic skill developed overtime to foster results.

I encourage all budding entrepreneurs to look within their communities to find programs they can leverage to get started. Many States provide funding, programs, incubators, and grants to help you get your business off the ground. A great place to start is the Small Business Administration website and look at the resources available to you locally.

Scan the QR code to visit the Small Business Administration.

End of Chapter Checklist

    Who needs to know about my business?

    Who would champion my business?

    Who can help my business?

GO!

*For God hath not give us the spirit
of fear but of power and of love and
of sound mind... 2 Timothy 1-7*

My intention with this book was to provide a 30,000-foot view of the tasks entrepreneurs have to tackle when they embark on their journey. There is no book that will prepare you completely for what you will encounter everyday. The challenges, the difficulties, frustrations and exhilarations. Entrepreneurship is for the bold and the risk takers. The ones that bet on themselves but who are not all about themselves. It is never too late to start nor is it too early. It is about the right time.

My hope is that you are successful. Do not be ashamed if you fail the first, second, or tenth time. Thomas Edison famously said, "I have not failed. I've just found 10,000 ways that won't work." That is the mindset you must have. The number one thing that you need is the mindset never to give up. It sounds cliché but it is true. It is easier to deal with the failures of life than to live with regrets.

Back in 2016, I created a welcome statement for new employees. I had it printed on a quality notecard to be displayed on their desk. It resonated back in 2016 and as it does today. I leave you with it as you head out on your way.

*The only thing that guarantees sustainability is growth. The way we foster that growth is through work. Meaningful work that give us **pride and purpose**. **Excitement** and **anxiousness**. Work that you can call your own. The kind of work that warrants sacrifice and taking a chance. Do not be afraid to standout, take chances, and make a mistake. Growth is what happens when you do.*

Be ready to work. Be ready to grow.

THE STARTING BLUPRNT CHECKLIST

Task
Description of Business
Mission Statement
Vision Statement
Core Values
Articles of Incorporation
Any Required Licenses
Any Required Permits
Insurance Policy(s)
EIN Number
Operating Account
Merchant Account (If Needed)
Business Credit Card (If Needed)
Line of Credit (If Needed)
Completed Proforma
Logo

	Business Cards
	Website (Landing Page)
	Social Media Handles
	Google Workspace Account
	Email Set Up
	Total Addressable Market (TAM)
	Serviceable Addressable Market (SAM)
	Serviceable Obtainable Market (SOM)
	Marketing 4Ps
	SWOT Analysis
	Marketing Brochure
	CRM Software or Google Sheets
	Operational Strategy
	Communication Plan
	Customer Process Map
	Internal Process Map
	HR/Payroll Software (If Needed)
	Employee Training Materials (If Needed)
	Employee Handbook (If Needed)
	Worker's Compensation Insurance (If Needed)
	Start Up Capital

THE STARTING BLUPRNT - FUN STUFF

My Top Business Movies:

    Godfather I/II
    War Dogs
    Scarface
    American Gangster
    The Founder
    Margin Call
    The Big Short
    Belly
    Lamborghini

My Top TV Series/Docuseries/Documentaries:

    The Men Who Built America
    The Smartest Guys in the Room
    General Magic
    Inside Bill's Brain
    Shark Tank
    American Greed

My Top Podcasts

    Acquired
    The GaryVee Experience
    American Greed Podcast
    McKinsey Talks Operations

HBR IdeaCast

Don't forget the Wall Street Journal!

www.ingramcontent.com/pod-product-compliance
Lightning Source LLC
Chambersburg PA
CBHW070350230526
45471CB00006B/2501